EXPLORATION THROUGH THE AGES

THE VOYAGES
OF COLUMBUS

Richard Humble

Illustrated by
Richard Hook

Franklin Watts
London · New York · Toronto · Sydney

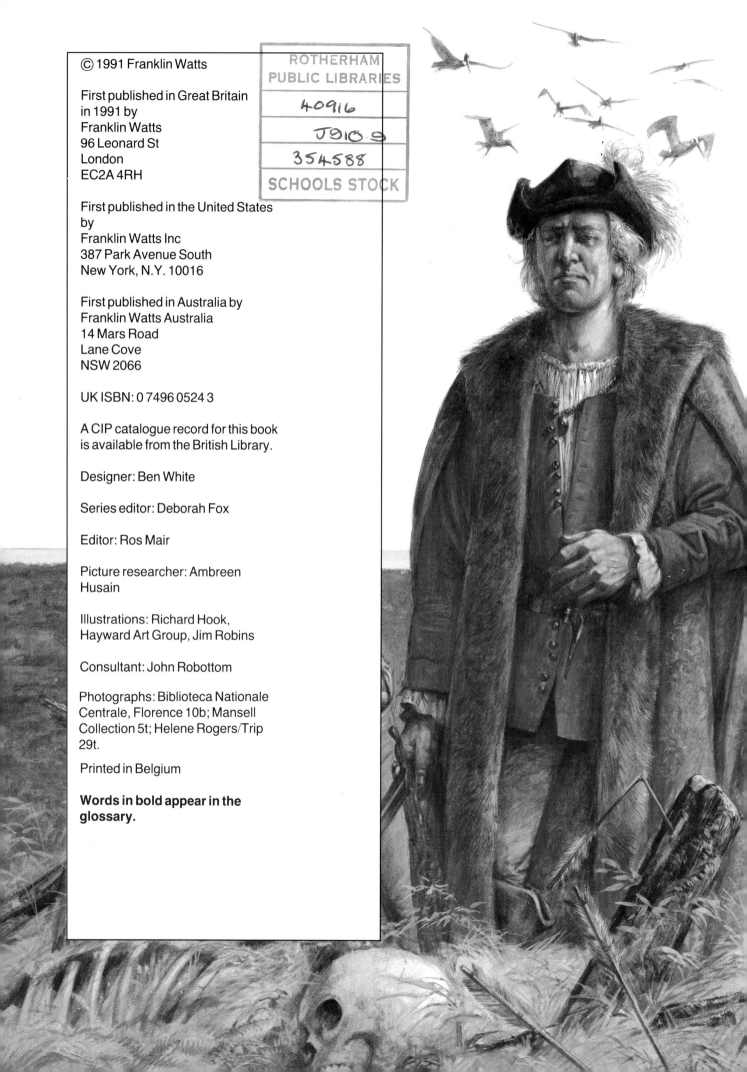

© 1991 Franklin Watts

First published in Great Britain
in 1991 by
Franklin Watts
96 Leonard St
London
EC2A 4RH

First published in the United States
by
Franklin Watts Inc
387 Park Avenue South
New York, N.Y. 10016

First published in Australia by
Franklin Watts Australia
14 Mars Road
Lane Cove
NSW 2066

UK ISBN: 0 7496 0524 3

A CIP catalogue record for this book
is available from the British Library.

Designer: Ben White

Series editor: Deborah Fox

Editor: Ros Mair

Picture researcher: Ambreen
Husain

Illustrations: Richard Hook,
Hayward Art Group, Jim Robins

Consultant: John Robottom

Photographs: Biblioteca Nationale
Centrale, Florence 10b; Mansell
Collection 5t; Helene Rogers/Trip
29t.

Printed in Belgium

**Words in bold appear in the
glossary.**

Contents

West by sea to China?

Why did it take until the year 1492 for European explorers to make the first ocean voyage across the Atlantic and back?

One good reason was that before the 15th century, European ships were too primitive for long-distance ocean voyages. The open longships of the Vikings, 500 years before, had certainly been capable of reaching North America, but only by "hopping" – they made a number of shorter voyages, from Ireland to Iceland, from Iceland to Greenland, and from Greenland to the North American coast.

Apart from not having the right ships for the ocean crossing, most European ship-owners of the Middle Ages made their money from trading voyages to known ports and markets, mostly in the eastern Mediterranean Sea. It was from here that the richest cargoes of all, the silks and spices from the Far East, were shipped to European markets after their long journey over land and sea.

Some tough Europeans had made that journey, returning with thrilling tales of the wealth and marvels of the Far East. One of the most famous of them, Marco Polo of Venice, wrote a detailed book about his travels in **Cathay**, the Chinese Empire of **Kublai Khan**. He had also described the rich island of "Cipangu" (Japan). But by the early 15th century, 100 years after Marco Polo's death, the sea-trading links with the eastern Mediterranean had become closed to

Europeans by the rise of the Turkish Empire. If European merchants still wanted to get rich by shipping cargoes of Far Eastern luxury goods, new sea routes would have to be found outside the Turkish control of trade with Asia. The result was a new interest in what had been learned about the world since the great geographers of ancient times. And this knowledge was to be tested by expeditions in ships which were now big and fast enough to cope with long ocean voyages.

The first attempts were made by the

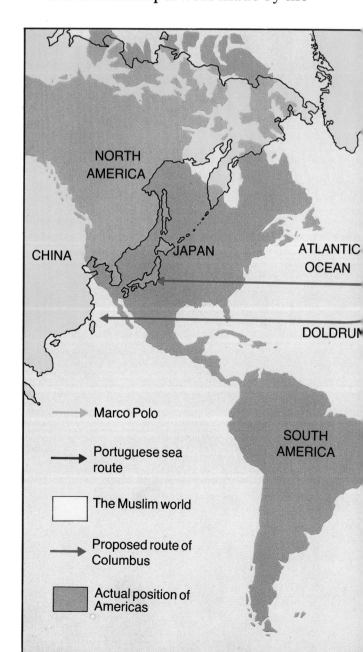

- → Marco Polo
- → Portuguese sea route
- ▢ The Muslim world
- → Proposed route of Columbus
- ▨ Actual position of Americas

▷ Columbus believed he could sail west across the Atlantic all the way to China, little knowing that the American continents lay in his path. He could not believe that the world was big enough for two new continents to block his path.

4

▷ By the late 15th century, the maps of the world available to seafarers and explorers like Columbus contained more guesses and imagination than accurate or useful information. Produced in 1491, the year before Columbus sailed, this is the world map of the German geographer Martin Behaim (about 1437-1507). It was designed to be wrapped around a wooden globe.

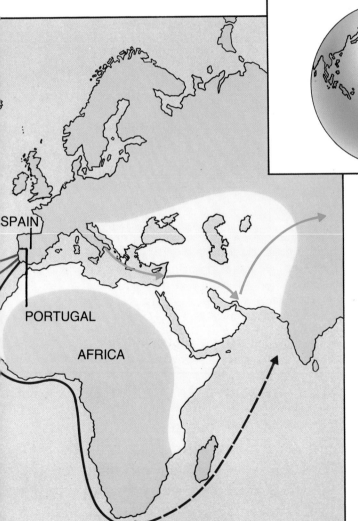

◁ The small map shows the world as Columbus imagined it to be. It is many thousands of miles too small, with the known continents – Europe and Asia – many thousands of miles too big, and the Atlantic Ocean far too narrow.

Portuguese, pushing further and further down Africa's Atlantic coast to find how far south the great continent extended. But by 1480 over 8,000 kilometres (5,000 miles) of Africa's west coast had been explored with no sign of any sea route around Africa to the east. The riches of China, Japan and "the Indies" seemed as far away as ever.

It was now that the idea began to grow that it might be easier to reach China by sailing *west*, across the Atlantic. In 1485 there came to the court of Spain a sailor who was convinced that the Atlantic route could be found, and who asked for ships and crews to prove it. His name was Christopher Columbus.

5

The man from Genoa

Christopher Columbus was an Italian, born in the sea-trading republic of Genoa in 1451. His father Domenico was a merchant in the business of making and selling woollen cloth, but with no seafaring tradition.

Little is known about the early life of Columbus. With his brothers Bartolomeo, Giovanni, and Giacomo, he was brought up to work at his father's trade, for which he was taught to read and write. But Christopher was not content to spend his life in the family business. Long before he was 20 years old, he had decided to spend his life at sea.

In 1502 Columbus wrote: "From a very small age I went sailing upon the sea and have continued to this day, which very occupation inclines all who follow it to wish to learn the secrets of the world." He may have made his first short voyages as young as 14, but by the early 1470s he was sailing as far as Tunis in North Africa and Chios in the Greek islands.

By 1478 Columbus had made his first voyages out into the Atlantic, one to Iceland by way of Ireland, followed by a sugar-buying voyage to the island of Madeira. He was living in Lisbon, in Portugal, working for the Genoese merchants of the Centurione family. He married the daughter of a Madeira landowner. By 1481 he was making voyages down the coast of Portuguese West Africa.

During these adventures Columbus learned the science of ocean navigation and read widely, studying works of geography and travel like the famous book of Marco Polo. He became convinced that

▷ In January 1492 Columbus gets his "miracle", as the Queen's messenger summons him back to court. "Everyone else was disbelieving," he later wrote, "but to the Queen, my Lady, God gave the spirit of understanding."

Cipangu (Japan) could be reached by sailing west across the Atlantic, but King John II of Portugal refused to give Columbus ships with which to prove it.

In 1485 Columbus moved to Spain, and spent seven weary years presenting his plan at the court of King Ferdinand and Queen Isabella. It seemed to him like a miracle when, having left the court in despair, he was called back in January 1492 to be given his chance at last.

Columbus's ships

The little fleet provided by Spain for the Atlantic adventure of Columbus in 1492 consisted of two small **caravels**, *Pinta* and *Nina*, and a larger, slower-sailing storeship, *Santa Maria*.

For over 30 years before Columbus sailed from Spain in August 1492, the Portuguese had proved that the type of ship best suited for ocean voyaging was the caravel: a small, three or four-masted ship which took a crew of about 35. The caravel carried the triangular or

△ *Santa Maria*, a small trading ship, or *nao*, was the flagship in which Columbus sailed on his first voyage in August 1492. She was the fleet storeship.

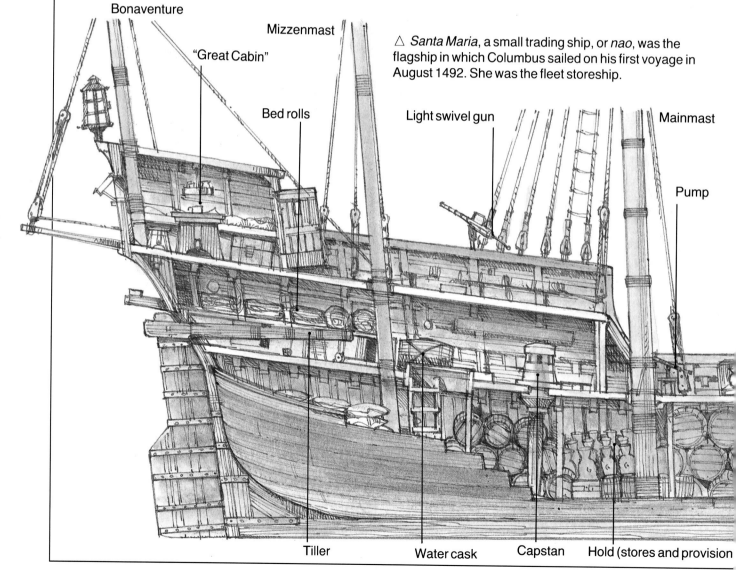

Bonaventure

Mizzenmast

"Great Cabin"

Bed rolls

Light swivel gun

Mainmast

Pump

Tiller

Water cask

Capstan

Hold (stores and provision

lateen sail adopted from the Arabs, which enabled a ship to sail close to the wind. Caravels could also be re-**rigged** to carry **square sails** for running before prevailing winds, such as the **trade winds** of the Atlantic. Columbus was relying on these winds to carry him across the ocean. *Nina* was re-rigged in this way before the main Atlantic

△ *Santa Maria*, at left, with the caravel *Nina* (at centre, with square main sail) and *Pinta*, shown with the triangular lateen-sail rig.

crossing began. The crew were to be closely confined on their voyage. There was only limited cabin space for the officers in the stern. The men slept forward, sheltered by the foredeck.

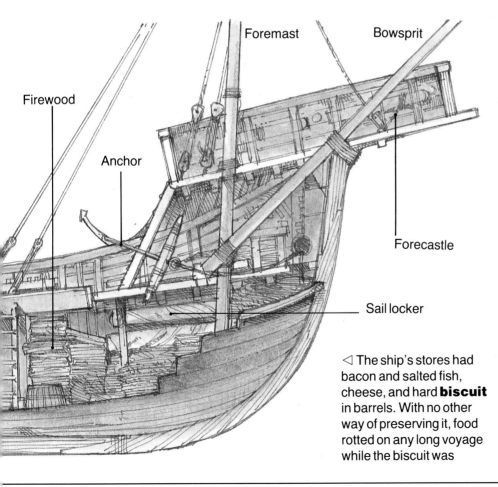

Firewood

Anchor

Foremast

Bowsprit

Forecastle

Sail locker

◁ The ship's stores had bacon and salted fish, cheese, and hard **biscuit** in barrels. With no other way of preserving it, food rotted on any long voyage while the biscuit was

eaten by weevils. Cooking (by boiling) was done in an iron firebox on the upper deck, with a bucket of water kept handy to put out any accidental fires.
　Instruments for navigation were few and primitive: a compass to give the ship's direction or heading; an **astrolabe** to measure the height or altitude of the Sun or stars in the sky, which gave the ship's north-south latitude; and constantly-turned hour-glasses to time each stage of the ship's run, and so work out the ship's east-west longitude. With these crude tools, navigators were forced to use the technique of "dead reckoning" – estimating their position from the ship's course, speed, and likely drift **downwind**.

Moment of decision

Columbus sailed from Palos in Spain on 3 August 1492. The crews of *Santa Maria*, *Pinta* and *Nina*, recruited in Palos and Seville, numbered fewer than 100 men in all. They included prison convicts who had been offered a royal pardon if they volunteered.

After taking on more supplies in the **Canaries** and converting *Nina* to a square-sail rig, the three little ships set off into the unknown on 6 September, with the easterly trade wind at their sterns.

Though the weather was fair and the following wind remained steady, the crews became more and more anxious that they would never find a wind to carry them home to Spain. A day of winds from the west on 22 September helped calm their fears, but this did not last long.

Columbus used many tricks to persuade his men to keep going. He faked the ship's log, telling the men that they had sailed fewer miles per day than he believed they had. (In fact, Columbus, always over-hopeful in his calculations, was actually giving them a truer account of the distance travelled than he thought.) And Columbus tried to cheer the men by claiming that every bird they sighted, every piece of floating wood or shower of rain, was a certain sign that land could no longer be far away.

By the end of the first week of October, however, the men had had enough. They would no longer listen to Columbus's promises of the riches of Cipangu (Japan). On 9 October he turned to the south, praying for a landfall on the coast of China. Now Columbus needed all his strength of will and faith in God. Without an early miracle, he knew the voyage would surely end in mutiny and failure.

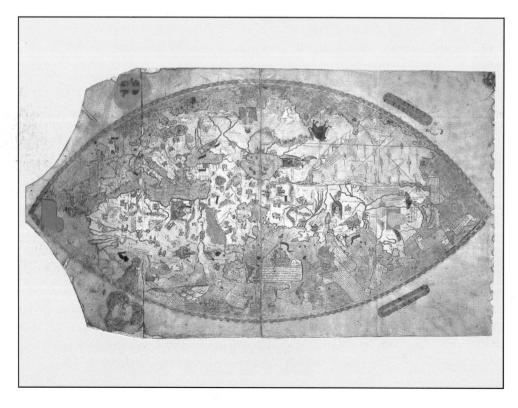

◁ The **planisphere** or world map of the Italian Pietro Paolo Toscanelli, c. 1480. The belief that there was a direct ocean route from Europe west to China encouraged Columbus in his great project. Toscanelli's map shows open sea between Spain and Africa (at left) and China (at extreme right).

▷ Thirty-five days after their last sight of land in the Canaries, *Santa Maria*'s crew demand to return home to Spain. Columbus encourages them to carry on by claiming that passing seagulls are birds from nearby land.

Land!

△ 12 October 1492: *Santa Maria*, *Pinta* and *Nina* sail close to the shore of the first island discovered west of the open Atlantic, to which Columbus gave the name of San Salvador.

The change of course southwards, and more convincing signs of land including a stick which had clearly been carved, encouraged the men to sail on for another two days. And then, 37 days out from the Canaries, at 2 o'clock in the night on Friday, 12 October 1492, seaman Rodrigo de Triana aboard the *Pinta* raised the cry of *"Tierra! Tierra!"* ("Land! Land!"). Ahead of the little fleet lay the low cliffs of an island, gleaming white in the moonlight. Prayers of thanks to God were said in all three ships.

Columbus landed in the morning, planting the royal banner of Spain and claiming the island in the names of King Ferdinand and Queen Isabella. Shy but friendly, the native islanders came out to greet the strangers. Columbus was surprised to see that they wore no clothes. These were clearly not the rich people of the East of whom Marco Polo had written. Columbus decided that he had reached one of the 1,500 islands lying east of China mentioned by Polo. From the islanders' chatter he learned that they called their home "Guanahani". Columbus named it San Salvador, after Christ the Saviour.

Columbus was delighted with the climate and the plants which grew so abundantly, and he noted that San Salvador would make a fine colony for Spain. The gentle islanders would, he

believed, become Christians and work willingly for their new rulers. Above all, there was hope of a big island not far away. Some of the islanders wore small ornaments of gold, which, they claimed, by sign language, came from a bigger island. In search of this gold, Columbus determined to sail on, to explore the maze of islands which could be seen on the southern horizon, beyond which he hoped to find China.

For many years it was believed that San Salvador was Watling Island in the southern **Bahamas**. But modern computer research, matching the account of Columbus with known winds and tides, has shown that his first landfall was more probably Samana Cay, which lies further to the south-east.

▽ The first crossing of the Atlantic by Columbus (6 September-12 October 1492) used the steady trade winds blowing west from the Canaries and made landfall in the southern Bahamas.

Columbus naturally believed that the islands that he had found were some of those which Marco Polo had mentioned as lying east of China. Columbus called them the "Indies".

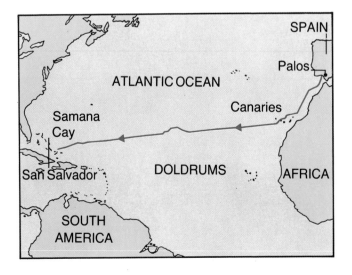

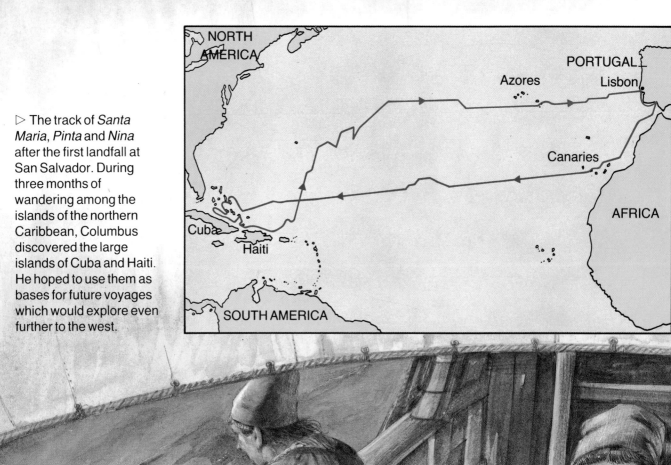

▷ The track of *Santa Maria*, *Pinta* and *Nina* after the first landfall at San Salvador. During three months of wandering among the islands of the northern Caribbean, Columbus discovered the large islands of Cuba and Haiti. He hoped to use them as bases for future voyages which would explore even further to the west.

Among the islands

For nearly three months after the discovery of San Salvador, Columbus steered his ships cautiously through the maze of reefs and small islands which lay to the south. He gave the names of the King and Queen to "Fernandina" (Long Island) and "Isabela" (Crooked Island), and he sighted the long, wooded shore of Cuba – an island so big that Columbus was convinced that it must be part of the Chinese mainland.

From the friendly islanders, with whom he traded cheap trinkets for their gold ornaments, he learned of a war-like tribe, the Caribs, who ate the flesh of their bravest enemies. It is after these people that the **Caribbean** Sea is named.

Christmas was approaching when *Santa Maria* was wrecked by night off the coast of Columbus's most important island discovery. This was Haiti, to the east of Cuba, which he named the "Spanish Island" (*La Española*, or *Hispaniola*). But Columbus did not lose heart. He landed, exchanged gifts of friendship with Guacanagari, the most powerful chief on the coast, and used wood from the wreck of *Santa Maria* to build a small fort, Navidad. This was an important moment in the history of the world, for Navidad was the first attempt by Europeans to establish a colony in the islands west of the Atlantic Ocean.

Leaving a force of 39 men at Navidad with orders to collect gold from the islanders until he returned, Columbus set sail for Spain with *Pinta* and *Nina* in January 1493, carrying gold samples and a group of frightened "Indians".

◁ Meeting of two worlds. On the deck of *Santa Maria*, curious islanders feel the strange clothes of Columbus and his men and willingly exchange their gold ornaments for cheap Spanish trinkets such as little bells. Spanish crewmen examine a *canoa*, adding the word for canoe to their language.

Home on the wings of storm

Though his men had always been fearful that Columbus would lead them so far to the west that they would never see Spain again, Columbus had always known how he would return. From his earlier voyages to the **Azores**, he knew of the powerful winds of the North Atlantic which sweep towards the coasts of Europe from the south-west. After sailing from Haiti, Columbus therefore sailed north, not east, on the first stage of his return voyage to Spain across the Atlantic.

But even Columbus, great seaman though he was, had never felt the terrible strength of the storms in the North Atlantic. Unlike the easy sailing of the outward voyage, the return to Europe was a storm-driven nightmare all the way. Columbus, in *Nina*, lost contact with *Pinta* after the two ships were driven apart in a gale. Non-stop storms badly damaged *Nina*'s masts and rigging, and made it next to impossible for Columbus to take sightings in order to work out his likeliest position in these unknown seas.

In the face of all these odds, Columbus brought the storm-battered *Nina* to anchor off Santa Maria in the Azores on 18 February 1493 – but even then his troubles were not over. The Portuguese suspected this strange Spanish ship in their waters to be a pirate, and ten Spaniards who went ashore to offer prayers of thanks were thrown in jail before Columbus secured their release. He had to cope with more storms on the last stage of the voyage home, and when he reached Lisbon in March he was sternly questioned by his old patron, King John II of Portugal. But at last, in April 1493, Columbus stood before the King and Queen of Spain, presenting his "Indians" and samples of gold at the court in Barcelona.

It seemed as if his luck could not hold; Columbus was far from pleased to hear that *Pinta* had also succeeded in reaching Spain safely. Throughout the voyage, Columbus and the captain of *Pinta*, Martin Pinzon, had disagreed time and again, and Pinzon was likely to tell a very different story from the glowing picture painted by Columbus. But the terrible strain of surviving the North Atlantic storms had been too much for Pinzon. He died after landing in Spain, leaving Columbus to tell his story unchallenged.

The return to Spain from this astonishing first voyage across the Atlantic was the greatest moment of Columbus's life. The Spanish King and Queen loaded him with honours and titles, and ordered a second voyage to be prepared. The man from Genoa, the Italian with the crazy dreams, had become "Don Cristobal Colon, Admiral of the Ocean Sea, Viceroy and Governor of the Islands newly discovered in the West". The fame of Columbus and his voyage spread across Europe, astonishing those who had believed that the only ocean route was the one around Africa which the Portuguese had not yet completed.

◁ Another massive wave crashes across the deck of the reeling *Nina* as the gallant caravel stands up to yet another North Atlantic storm. The fact that *Nina* survived the terrible return voyage to Spain, to make at least two more crossings of the Atlantic, shows the amazing endurance of these small ships, and their value to the men who made the first voyages of world exploration in unknown seas.

Return to Hispaniola

The second voyage of Columbus was on a far larger scale than the first, with a fleet of 17 ships (including the trusty *Nina*) and over 1,300 men. Their task was to settle a colony on Hispaniola, and to continue the exploration of the new lands in the west.

Choosing a more southerly track for his second Atlantic crossing, Columbus arrived off the newly-found island of Dominica, in the Lesser **Antilles**, on 3 November 1493 – a crossing of only 29 days. Using his wonderful navigating instinct, he steered north and west by way of Puerto Rico and Guadaloupe, reaching Hispaniola on 22 November.

Here he was greeted by the chief Guacanagari with news of disaster. The 39

Spaniards left at Navidad ten months before had all been killed, and the fort burned to the ground. It was a daunting return to the islands, but Columbus sensibly refused demands to punish the Indians. Indeed he made peace with them, and set about the settlement of the new colony. On 24 April 1494 he sailed west from Hispaniola to resume the work of exploration.

South-west of Hispaniola, Columbus had hoped to find the Chinese mainland.

▽ Resplendent in his new rank as "Viceroy of the Indies", Columbus stares aghast at the results of the first attempted settlement – the dead bodies of his men lie scattered among the ruins of the fort of Navidad on Hispaniola.

Instead he discovered another island, Jamaica, and a wide sea passage leading to the south coast of Cuba. Rather than admit that he had been wrong, Columbus lost his nerve, making his men swear on oath that Cuba was not an island.

Returning to Hispaniola brought no comfort. The new colony, Isabela, had an unhealthy climate. There was little gold, the Spaniards were fighting the natives, and they hated Columbus for having lied to bring them there. After shifting the colony west to the new site of Santo Domingo, Columbus sailed for Spain in the early summer of 1496, to explain his failures to the King and Queen, and defend himself against his many critics.

A new world

Though Ferdinand and Isabella did not agree with Columbus's ideas about how the Hispaniola colony should be run, they had not lost faith in their "Admiral of the Ocean Sea". But Columbus sailed on his third voyage in the summer of 1498 knowing that his position was bound to suffer if he did not discover lands as rich in gold as those he had originally promised.

Columbus therefore made his third Atlantic crossing (July 1498) further south than ever before, believing that the best gold-bearing lands were to be found in the heat of the Tropics. He and his men suffered greatly from the heat as they cruised through the **Doldrums**, between the north and south Atlantic trade winds. But on 31 July 1498 they reached the island of Trinidad, southernmost island of the Caribbean.

The greatest of all Columbus's discoveries was only a few days away: the continent of South America, and the mouth of a river so huge – the River Orinoco – that it turned the water of the sea fresh. After two weeks of exploring the coast around the Gulf of **Paria**, Columbus wrote in his journal (14 August 1498): "I believe that this is a very large continent which until now has remained unknown."

Columbus had little time to spare for exploring the new continent, for he was expected in Hispaniola. He made a wonderfully accurate voyage from Paria across the Caribbean direct to Santo Domingo – but once back in Hispaniola his troubles began in earnest.

Columbus and his brothers, whom he had brought to help him govern the colony, were hated by the Spanish colonists, who rebelled against his rule. Complaints against the misrule of the "Italians" were sent to Ferdinand and Isabella until, in the summer of 1500, the King and Queen felt obliged to act. They sent Francisco de Bobadilla to Hispaniola to investigate the complaints and take over as governor if he thought fit. On arriving in Hispaniola, Bobadilla had the Columbus brothers arrested and shipped back to Spain in irons to be tried. It was the worst moment of Columbus's life, but it was not the end of his career. Even after this shameful homecoming, Columbus was to be given one last chance to prove that he was neither a criminal nor mad.

◁ First steps in the New World: Columbus lands to claim Paria (in modern Venezuela) for Spain.

▽ The third voyage of Columbus, showing his remarkable passage from Paria to Hispaniola.

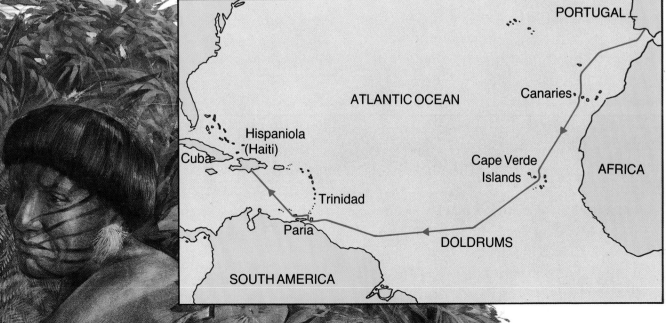

Ordeal of the "High Voyage"

Once back in Spain Columbus was immediately released, but Ferdinand and Isabella refused to restore him as governor of Hispaniola. He could not return to the group of islands until a new governor had been chosen for Hispaniola, where Columbus was now forbidden to land. The new governor, Nicolas de Ovando, did not sail for Hispaniola until February 1502. Only then was Columbus permitted to sail on his fourth voyage.

Columbus called it his "High Voyage" – a daring gamble in which he hoped to win back all he had lost. He planned to sail between the Caribbean islands and the new continent discovered in the south, and so win through to China at last.

Sailing from Spain in April 1502, Columbus made his fastest-ever Atlantic crossing: 21 days from the Canaries to the Indies. But this good luck did not last. He tried to put in at Hispaniola, not only to take on supplies but to warn Ovando that all the weather signs showed that a hurricane was coming. But Ovando refused to listen, and ordered a fleet to set sail for Spain while Columbus and his four caravels took shelter in a small bay. Though Columbus's ships survived the hurricane, 19 of Ovando's ships were lost, along with over 500 men.

With Hispaniola still closed to him, Columbus sailed west and south across the Caribbean until, at the end of July 1502, he reached the American coast again at the eastern end of the Gulf of **Honduras**. From here he decided to follow the coast to the east, to discover whether it joined up with his earlier mainland discovery at Paria.

Weary weeks turned into months as

Columbus followed the American coast, east and then south along the shores of modern Nicaragua and Costa Rica, hoping against hope to find a sea channel leading south and west. Fighting foul weather and torrential rain, the likes of which Columbus had never seen before, the ships crept eastward towards the **Isthmus** of Panama. This slender strip of unbroken land wrecked Columbus's last despairing hopes of reaching the Indies by sea to the west. He had to accept that there was no strait or sea passage which would carry his ships onward to win the riches of China.

▷ Lashed by merciless rain, the ships of Columbus feel their way along the coast of Central America. "The crews were so oppressed," wrote Columbus, "that they wished for death to end their sufferings."

Shipwrecked on Jamaica

The end of 1502 found Columbus and his ships off the coast of Veragua (modern western Panama). Here explorations ashore found encouraging amounts of gold, which Columbus hoped would win him back to royal favour in Spain.

On 6 January 1503 the ships anchored in the Belem River, along whose valley large amounts of gold were found. Columbus tried to build a fort in which, as at Navidad ten years before, he would leave a garrison while he returned to send further supplies from Hispaniola. But now a new danger threatened. The hulls of the ships were becoming riddled with holes eaten by the sea worms that swarm in tropical waters. There was nothing for it but to sail at once for Hispaniola while the ships could still remain afloat.

On 1 May 1503, Columbus left the American coast for the last time. The fears of the men prevented him from steering

the easterly course he wanted, with the result that the ships reached the islands too far west, at Cuba. By now the ships were so badly worm-eaten that the pumps could no longer control the inward flood of seawater. A last desperate attempt to reach Hispaniola was beaten by unfavourable winds, and Columbus had no choice but to beach his sinking ships on the coast of Jamaica. The "High Voyage" had come to its end.

Weary and ill in both mind and body, Columbus had to endure a dreadful year marooned on Jamaica. Some of his men rebelled, and he had to fight a battle to defeat them. The native Arawaks attacked too. After months of these dangers, and poor food, Columbus's most loyal officer, Diego Mendez, made an epic voyage to Hispaniola in a native canoe to beg Ovando for help. Unless relief ships came, Columbus and his surviving men would be doomed to die on Jamaica.

Hard-hearted to the last, Ovando refused to send ships to rescue the castaways on Jamaica until the next supply fleet reached Hispaniola from Spain. Even then, more bad weather caused weeks of delay before Columbus was able to sail from Hispaniola to Spain, where he finally arrived on 7 November 1504 – to find that Queen Isabella was dying.

△ A desperate venture begins. Diego Mendez gives a last wave to Columbus and his men, marooned on the coast of Jamaica. Though the nearest Spanish settlement was over 720 kilometres (450 miles) from Jamaica, Mendez knew that the only hope of rescue for the castaways lay with their hostile fellow-countrymen on Hispaniola.

End of an epic life

Columbus was not yet 55 years old when he returned to Spain at the end of 1504, but the hardships he had suffered had made him old before his time. He never went to sea again.

His last 18 months of life were spent begging King Ferdinand to grant the money which Columbus insisted was his share of the profits of the Indies, and in making wilder and wilder claims about what he had actually discovered on his four famous voyages.

In his last years, Columbus found it hard to believe how much had changed since he had first set sail across the Atlantic in 1492. Led by Vasco da Gama, the Portuguese had finally succeeded (1499) in opening up the sea route to the east around Africa's southern tip. The western route across the Atlantic which Columbus had tried so hard to find seemed as far away as ever.

After the first voyage of Columbus, in 1494, Pope Alexander VI had divided the New World between Spain and Portugal. The Pope awarded all lands west of a north-south line down the central Atlantic to Spain, and all lands east to Portugal. Columbus found it very hard to accept that the Portuguese, sailing far out into the South Atlantic on their long voyages to southern Africa, had found that a large part of South America, which Columbus thought of as his, lay on the Portuguese side of the line. (This is the country known today as Brazil.)

As his death drew nearer, Columbus became almost desperate in his claims that he had, in fact, succeeded in reaching the seas of Asia. He revived his old, false claim

▽ The death of Columbus (20 May 1506). Diego Columbus gently closes his father's eyes as the priest recites the prayers for the dead.

that Cuba was no island, but part of the Chinese coastline. To admit that his New World, the American continent, was in fact a giant land barrier blocking the western sea route to Asia, was too much for him to bear.

At least, once King Ferdinand had granted the money due to Columbus from Hispaniola, the "Admiral of the Ocean Sea" ended his life a wealthy man.

Surrounded by his sons, Columbus died at his home in Seville on 20 May 1506, and the Spanish court records did not even trouble to mention his death. It could be said that in death the great explorer continued his travels, for despite a splendid tomb built in Seville Cathedral, his body lay at Santo Domingo from 1556 to 1795 before his ashes went home to his "beloved Genoa".

The Spanish legacy

In his amazing life, Christopher Columbus dreamed many dreams which could never come true. But perhaps the saddest of those dreams concerned the people he discovered west of the Atlantic: the Indians of the Caribbean and the American mainland, for whom discovery by Spain meant a cruel new life under Spanish rule.

Columbus was neither cruel nor a tyrant. He really believed that Spanish rule would be good for the Indians. Columbus promised King Ferdinand and Queen Isabella that he could "make them work, sow seed and do whatever else is necessary and build a town and teach them to wear clothes and adopt our

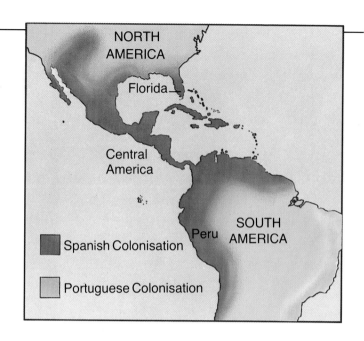

△ Within 50 years of the death of Columbus, further exploration and expeditions of conquest in Central and South America had won Spain a huge colonial empire stretching from Peru to Florida.

▷ Watched over by armed guards, black slaves shipped across the Atlantic from Africa labour in the fields of a Hispaniola plantation under the lash of their Spanish taskmasters.

customs".

But the Spaniards who sailed to the new lands in the Indies had other ideas. They saw the Indians as human animals, to be reduced to slaves and worked until they died for the good of their new masters. The Indians, who had never been used to hard work, made useless slaves. Instead of becoming dutiful workers, they died by the thousand. And if in despair they tried to fight their Spanish masters, even more Indians were killed in battle or massacred afterwards to teach the survivors a lesson.

The destruction of the Caribbean Indians did not make the Spaniards give up and go home. Instead, as Spain's new

△ A palace fit for a Spanish viceroy. Named after Columbus but built in 1509, three years after he died, this is the splendid Alcazar de Colon which still stands in the Dominican Republic – discovered by Columbus on his second voyage.

empire spread into South America and north into Mexico, they sought elsewhere for slave workers. So began the dreadful trade in black slaves from Africa, seized from their homes and shipped across the Atlantic to work in the mines and in the fields of the New World. The first shipload of black African slaves was landed in the Indies in 1501, before Columbus had sailed on his last voyage.

The saddest legacy of the discoveries of Columbus was therefore the African slave trade, which lasted nearly 350 years before it was finally banned.

Glossary

Antilles Chain of islands from Cuba to Trinidad, enclosing the Caribbean Sea.

Astrolabe Navigator's instrument for measuring the altitude, or height, of the Sun and stars, to calculate the ship's north-south latitude.

Azores Atlantic island group 1,450 kilometres (900 miles) west of Lisbon, discovered between 1427-31.

Bahamas Chain of islands about 250 kilometres (155 miles) north-east of Cuba; Columbus's first landfall west of the Atlantic in 1492.

Biscuit Flat cakes of hard bread baked from flour and water, made to feed ships' crews.

Canaries Atlantic island group 900 kilometres (560 miles) south of Spain and 150 kilometres (95 miles) from the north-west African coast.

Caravel Small, three or four-masted Mediterranean sailing ship, used on all major voyages of exploration from about 1420-1510.

Caribbean Sea between the Antilles island chain and the mainland of Central and South America, named after the cannibal tribe of the Caribs discovered by Columbus.

Cathay European name for China until the 16th century, made famous by Marco Polo.

Doldrums Belt of hot, still calm between the trade winds of the northern

▷ The four voyages of Columbus added mightily to the map of the world: all the major islands of the West Indies, the existence of the South American continent, and the long stretch of Central American coast stretching west and north from Panama around the Gulf of Mexico.

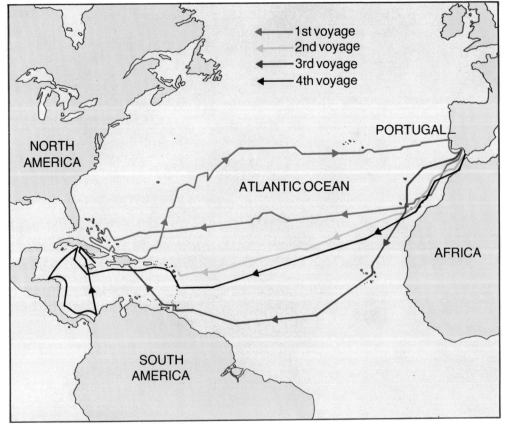

Timechart

and southern hemispheres.

Downwind In the direction blown by the wind (west is downwind of an east wind).

Honduras East-west coast of Central America between Yucatan and Panama, reached by Columbus in July 1502.

Isthmus Narrow stretch of land between two seas.

Kublai Khan Mongol Emperor of China (Cathay), visited by Marco Polo between 1274 and 1293.

Lateen Triangular fore-and-aft sail, enabling ships to sail close to the wind instead of running before it.

Log Day-to-day official record of a ship's progress, navigation and crew activities.

Paria South American bay (in modern Venezuela) discovered by Columbus in August 1498.

Planisphere Early name for "world map" (modern planispheres map the heavens).

Rigging All ropes and cables used to support a ship's masts and yards, and to hoist, trim, and lower sails.

Square-sail rig Rig of sails best suited for long runs before a following wind.

Trade winds Steady, regular ocean winds which blow towards the Equator – north-east trades above the Equator, south-east trades below – separated by the Doldrums.

1451 Christopher Columbus is born in Genoa, Italy.

1485 Columbus comes to Spain seeking ships and crews for his Atlantic venture.

1488 Bartholomew Diaz of Portugal discovers Africa's southern tip.

1492-93 First voyage of Columbus discovers the Bahamas, Cuba and Hispaniola (Haiti).

1493-96 Second voyage of Columbus discovers Dominica, Guadaloupe, Puerto Rico and Jamaica.

1497 John Cabot, sailing from Bristol, England, discovers Newfoundland.

1498 Third voyage of Columbus discovers Trinidad and South American mainland (Paria).

1498-99 Vasco da Gama of Portugal makes his first voyage to India around Africa.

1500 Vicente Pinzon and Pedro Alvarez of Portugal discover Brazil. Columbus is arrested and sent back to Spain in chains.

1502-3 Fourth voyage of Columbus follows Central American coast from Honduras to Panama.

1503-4 Columbus is stranded on Jamaica, awaiting rescue. November 1504 Columbus returns to Spain.

20 May 1506 Death of Columbus.

Index